Curious Sam

FELIPE COFREROS, Ph.D.

Order this book online at www.trafford.com
or email orders@trafford.com

Most Trafford titles are also available at major online book retailers.

Print information available on the last page.

ISBN: 978-1-4907-9215-6 (sc)
           978-1-4907-9216-3 (e)

Because of the dynamic nature of the Internet, any web addresses or links contained in this book may have changed since publication and may no longer be valid. The views expressed in this work are solely those of the author and do not necessarily reflect the views of the publisher, and the publisher hereby disclaims any responsibility for them.

Our mission is to efficiently provide the world's finest, most comprehensive book publishing service, enabling every author to experience success. To find out how to publish your book, your way, and have it available worldwide, visit us online at www.trafford.com

Any people depicted in stock imagery provided by Getty Images are models,
and such images are being used for illustrative purposes only.
Certain stock imagery © Getty Images.

Trafford rev. 11/12/2018

 www.trafford.com

North America & international
toll-free: 1 888 232 4444 (USA & Canada)
fax: 812 355 4082

Sam, a dog, and Ronie, a pony, are best friends. They play and run around the farm. They are always together.

One day while running, Sam and Ronie see something on a branch of a tree. They stop and stare at it. "What's that? Is it a fruit?" Sam asks Ronie. "It doesn't look like a fruit," Ronie answered.

Sam jumps to reach it, but he cannot. It is too high for him. "I can't reach it," he says. "Let me try," says Ronie, "I can reach higher than you."

Ronie jumps high trying to reach it, but he can't. "Oh, I can't reach it," Ronie says. He tries again but fails.

"I got it!" Sam shouts. He picks a stone and shows it to Ronie. "We'll throw stones at it," he says. "Okay. Let's do it." Ronie agrees.

Sam and Ronie throw stones at the object hanging on the branch of the tree. They laugh and shout as they do it. They enjoy throwing stones at it.

A stone hits the object. It breaks and bees come buzzing out of it. "Bees! It's a Beehive!" Sam shouts. "Run, Ronie, Run!"

Sam and Ronie run as fast as they can with the bees chasing them.

Exercise 1: Match the animal with its house.

1. dog   o   o

2. bees   o   o

3. horse   o   o

Exercise 2: Write the correct name below the pictures: Dog, Bee, Horse.

1. _____ 2. _____ 3. _____

Exercise 3: Yes or No

_____1. Sam and Ronie saw a fruit.

_____2.Sam and Ronie are best friends.

_____3.The bees run after Sam and Ronie.

_____4. The Bees live in a beehive.

_____5. Sam and Ronie run fast from the bees.

Exercise 4: Circle the correct answer.

1. Who is Sam's best friend?

    a. Tonie   b.Ronie   c.Roby

2. What is in the beehive?

    a. bees   b. a dog   c.a pony

3. Where was the beehve?

    a. It was on the ground under the tree.

    b. It was on the branch of the tree.

    c. It was on Sam's back.

4. What happened when the beehive broke?

    a. The bees flew out of it.

    b. The flowers bloomed from it.

    c. The leaves fell from it.

5. Why did Sam and Ronie stone the beehive?

    a. They like to throw stones.

    b. They want to know how they can hit the beehive.

    c. They want to know what they saw on the branch of the tree.

Exercise 5: Take Sam to his house.

Avoid the bees.

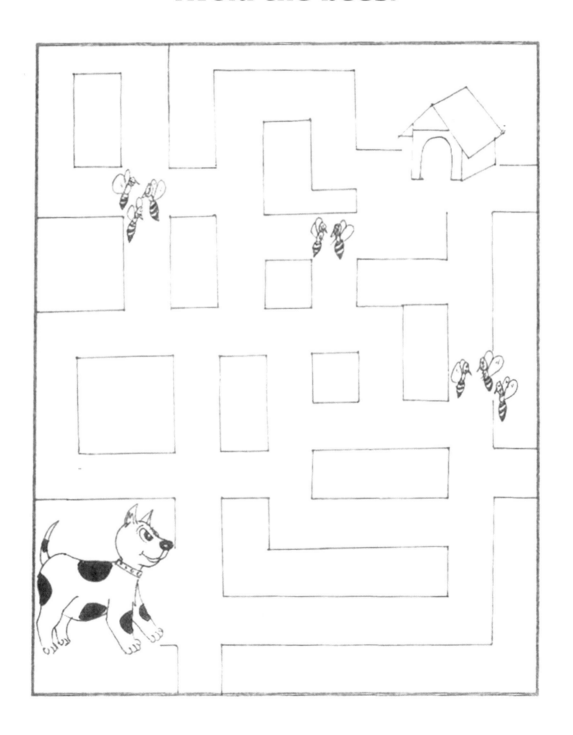

About the Author

Felipe Cofreros Ph.D. spent more than twenty-five years of aggregate experience in teaching Literacy, Adult Education, Pre-school, Elementary, High School, College and the administration of instructional English as a Second Language [ESL] services among Indo-Chinese refugees [Vietnamese, Lao, Khmer and Hmong] in the International Catholic Migration Commission [ICMC], Philippine Refugee Processing Center [PRPC] in Sabang, Morong, Bata-an, Philippines for a decade. Felipe also taught English as a Second Language [ESL] in different countries in Asia and North America. Presently, Felipe is one of the owners and the Executive Program Director of the International Adult Day Care in Las Vegas, Nevada, USA.

Felipe has authored more than a dozen of Children's Picture Books with comprehension questions for three years old and up geared for use in the preschool classroom; A Handbook of Basic Art, Part 1 [Painting Processes in Playing with Colors, Different Crayon Techniques]; A Handbook of Basic Art, Part 2 [Basic Drawing, Painting and Making Crafts]; Let's Weave [An ancient Hand Art

of Interlacing Two groups of Threads]; A Pre-school Math Workbook "Let's Build Our Math Skills Workbook for children ages three years old and up; Effective Ways To Assess English Language Learners [For Intermediate and Advanced Levels]; One Accord - an inspirational book of Bible promises; A Handbook of Writing Activities for Intermediate and Advanced English Language Learners and English Workbook 1, 2 and 3 for the Elementary level.

Felipe graduated as a scholar from the University of San Agustin in Iloilo City, Philippines with a Bachelor of Science in Elementary Education with specialization in Social Studies and Art Education. He also studied Basic Latin, Spanish and Theology courses in the Seminary of St. Augustine in Intramuros, Metropolitan Manila, Philippines. He got his Master's Degree in TESOL and Doctor of Philosophy in Sociology from an on-line University in the USA. Felipe obtained quite a number of certificates in different disciplines such as TESOL Teaching Certificate Course, Lingua Edge, LCC. TESOL Teaching Training Systems West Olympic Blvd., Beverly Hills, California, USA; Managing People for Maximum Performance in John F. Kennedy School of Management, Harvard University, Cambridge, Massachusetts, USA; The Roots of Learning: Society for Effective Affective Learning in Brighton, England, United Kingdom.

Printed in the United States
By Bookmasters